SCHIRMER'S LIBRARY
OF MUSICAL CLASSICS

Vol. 1580

WOLFGANG AMADEUS MOZART

Concerto No. 3
In G

For Violin and Piano

[K. 216]

Revision and Cadenzas by

SAM FRANKO

G. SCHIRMER, Inc.

DISTRIBUTED BY

HAL•LEONARD®
CORPORATION

7777 W. BLUEMOUND RD. P.O. BOX 13819 MILWAUKEE, WI 53213

Concerto in G
(K. 216)

Wolfgang Amadeus Mozart
Revision and cadenzas by Sam Franko

I

II

Violin

SCHIRMER'S LIBRARY
OF MUSICAL CLASSICS

Vol. 1580

Wolfgang Amadeus Mozart

Concerto No. 3
In G

For Violin and Piano

[K. 216]

Revision and Cadenzas by

SAM FRANKO

G. SCHIRMER, Inc.

DISTRIBUTED BY

HAL•LEONARD®
CORPORATION

7777 W. BLUEMOUND RD. P.O. BOX 13819 MILWAUKEE, WI 53213

Concerto in G

(K. 216)

Violin

Wolfgang Amadeus Mozart
Revision and cadenzas by Sam Franko

I

38751C

Violin

Violin

Violin

III

Rondeau
Allegro

III

Rondeau
Allegro